Advance Praise for *On the Farm, Down the Road*

In *On the Farm, Down the Road*, Ron Gower invites us to join him where "one thing leads to another." What the reader finds along the way is the deep affection of a life lived in being present to the moment. There is the occasional hilarity at the machinations of rural life: "Goat Proem" alone is worth the price of the book! But mostly the poems convey the sweet and tender heart of a man who celebrates the life of trout and grandchildren, maple trees and powdered ski slopes. These are deeply felt poems, and although death hovers ever-present down the "task/master fall line," there is such a brightness in the singing.

CARY WATERMAN
author of *The Salamander Migration* and *When I Looked Back You Were Gone*

୧୬

Ron Gower's poems remind me of browsing a photo album full of subjects about which I know next to nothing, and having a sudden revelation: Ah, this is *farming!* This is *fishing!* This is what living with *goats* is like! Some caused me to laugh out loud, while others made me cry. All of these poems, deftly written and deeply felt, reveal the photographer as a treasurer of history, a man of good humor and love. This is a collection to be read over and over again.

JUDITH GUEST
author of *Ordinary People* and *Second Heaven*

୧୬

Ron Gower has been diligently writing, editing, and teaching writers for all the years I've known him, so I've been waiting for this book for decades. His poems are full of self-knowledge without self-absorption. They observe and profoundly contemplate nature, work, friendship, death, and more—all related through acquaintance with family, neighbors, children, animals, and activity. The wisdom that emerges is rooted in farm work, passion for the outdoors, care for friends and family, and attention to great literature and music. As he teaches, so he is: Give Ron a chance, and he'll either heal your heart or steal it. Brilliantly!

JOHN CALVIN REZMERSKI
author of *What Do I Know?* and *Chin Music and Dirty Sermons*

On the Farm, Down the Road

ॐ

On the Farm, Down the Road

COLLECTED POEMS

ೞ

Ronald Gower

BLUEROAD PRESS
Janesville, Minnesota

On the Farm, Down the Road
Collected Poems
© 2010 Ronald H. Gower

ISBN13: 978-0-9796509-2-5
First Printing

❧

Blueroad Press
34402 15th Street
Janesville, Minnesota 56048

www.blueroadpress.com

John Gaterud, Editor & Publisher
Abbey Gaterud, Associate Editor

Book and cover design: John Gaterud
Cover and author photographs: John Cross

Printed on recycled paper in the United States by BookMobile, Minneapolis.

Many thanks to John Cross of *The Free Press* of Mankato, Minnesota, for his generosity on this project.

❧

To Anne Gower, my dear wife and best friend,
who has shared my life "On the Farm, Down the Road"
for fifty years.
No one could ask for better company
on this long trip than my beautiful "Queen Anne."

To Pat, Julie and family,
all my best to dear friends.
Hope you like these.

Ron Gower

Contents

Ah, (semi-) Wilderness!

WHEN MY WIFE, ANNE, AND I MOVED IN THE TUMULTUOUS
1970s to our small farm near Good Thunder, Minnesota,
it was not to escape the world, as was popular then.
We both had professions that we enjoyed: Anne was
a physical therapist, and I was an English professor.
Rather than isolating ourselves, we wanted to engage
our lives with more of the world, in more than could be
offered us in a city.

It is true that we wanted greater privacy and a reprieve
from crowds and the clang and rattle of busy streets;
we worked with people all day, and thought it healthier
for us (and them) to have time to ourselves. Our farm
was to be our castle: the Maple River forms our moat
on three sides, and the township road dead-ends at our
house. Anyone coming down the road is either lost — or
heading for our place.

The 17.92-acre tract that makes up our farm was
described rather generally in the first title abstract,

signed in 1864 by W. O. Stoddard, secretary to Abraham Lincoln. It proceeds from a survey marker "north up the Maple River to the large black maple tree," thence eastward to another marker across the river, and then south to the origin. In practical terms, it is everything from our driveway running east and west along the northern survey line to wherever the river flows on the other three sides. It is unlikely that the tract always measures 17.92 acres; in fact, it's probably a little different every year. I rather like to think of the river determining how much land we own, rather than the government.

In fact, it's hard to think in terms of ownership, looking through the abstract, with a dozen other "owners" listed since its inception, and Winnebago Indians as residents before that. It's a lovely, quiet place, and we're just glad to be the current inhabitants, enjoying what others have found here and passed on to us. I like to think that not much has really changed as I walk the woods around the farm, or hunt deer and turkey in the "neighborhood," or ski up the river in winter.

These are some of the more important reasons we moved, with our two small sons, to Maple Bend Farm. Although we both grew up in cities, Anne and I enjoy the outdoors and wildlife, and many of the things we wanted to do, outside our professions, were activities that required space and some level of autonomy. Living in a town is, quite simply, too restrictive in many ways, from where you can park your car to how you keep your

lawn, or whether you can let your dog run loose — or
your children, for that matter.

Among things we wanted were to have a dog (or dogs)
that could spend their lives outdoors without being
leashed, and to give our boys the kind of space that
would let them discover the natural world and invent
themselves. Elementary school was within walking
distance, and later the rural high school turned out to be
surprisingly good. Owen, our older son, was a National
Merit Scholar, and now works in semiconductors, while
Hugh is a firefighter and computer specialist. They
both return often to the farm — along with grandsons
Cade and Quinn, who revel in the open space and farm
activities as my sons did.

Besides a place to raise children, we wanted gardens and
orchards, some farm animals, and with them a greater
degree of self-sufficiency than we could find in a house
in the city. We had no illusions about being totally
self-supporting, but liked the idea of producing at least
some of our own food and living more in tune with
nature's cycles.

We plunged into projects and plans without any outside
help and often with more enthusiasm than knowledge.
Both of us grew up in cities and had to learn "country life"
as we went along. We cleared a huge garden space the first
year, in which Anne planted 88 tomato plants and equally
large plots of every other vegetable we could preserve

and consume. I built a root cellar, which served that purpose for ten years and then became a shelter for sheep. We raised a few of them every year, getting the benefit of their keeping the front lawn trimmed — and well-fertilized — as well as tasty lamb in the fall. There were also at various times chickens, geese, pheasant, and quail in residence, all interesting and all presenting challenges.

The most enchanting "livestock" were our honeybees. We gathered hundreds of pounds of liquid gold in the fifteen years we worked with bees, but that was only part of the attraction. Their intricate and complex societies kept us fascinated, as they have mankind throughout history — and prehistory. "Beekeeping" is a misnomer; we often felt the bees were the "keepers," as we followed their schedules and learned that they knew better what they were doing than we: the best beekeeping is the kind that interferes least with the colonies.

We supplemented our sweet-stock with maple syrup from the sugarbush that grew along the riverbank. Our method developed over the years, but was always small-scale and rather primitive compared to more serious syrup-makers; but we were not trying to make a business of it, only collecting and refining enough for our own needs and for a few friends.

And we hunted and gathered, from the raspberries that grew wild in our small woods-patch to the morels, shaggymanes, and other fungi that sprung up along the river. I've hunted deer regularly, with bow and arrow. My success has been limited, but most years there was more venison than beef in our freezer. I've had more luck with turkeys, and as with the venison we found wild turkey much tastier than the domestic version.

More important than the small additions to our larder was the time I spent afield. The land along the river is generally too flood-prone and hilly for cultivation, so I roamed for miles in what is essentially a wilderness. I've spent countless hours in tree-stands and blinds, watching the sun come up or go down, and enjoyed the company of raccoons, squirrels, fox, birds of all kinds, and the occasional deer or turkey.

I like to think that this is how the first "owners" of our land also enjoyed the fruits of the valley, and how the next residents will also benefit. We've tried to live on the land, not changing it in any significant way. For a few years, we rented the ten tillable acres to local farmers, who planted the usual corn and soybeans; but eventually we put that land in the Conservation Reserve Program and planted it in a mix of wild grasses and saplings. It's perfect habitat for wildlife of all kinds now, and the scene through our picture window overlooking the acreage is far more interesting than anything TV has to offer.

We were in some ways a little naïve — or just plain ignorant — about some of the demands this kind of life would make. When the shallow well froze up and left us without water, we had to get it running again — usually at twenty to thirty degrees below zero. If our driveway filled up with snow, blocking our way to the township road, we had to clear it ourselves; and if the tractor wouldn't start, that had to be fixed before we could plow. And when the river came over its banks in the spring, the beehives had to be moved — whether the bees liked it or not — before floodwaters drowned them out or carried them away. But that was the price we learned to pay for all the advantages of country life, and it was well worth it — as was the pride that always followed in solving one of those unforeseen problems.

We have lived on this small piece of land for more than thirty years now, and are both retired. Naturally, our activities and interests have changed, but we still find that this place offers us everything we want. We're not as ambitious: the garden has shrunk from a half-acre to a few raised beds, and we don't keep any animals except for our Springer Spaniel, Boots, who has grown old along with us. We have always fed the birds, and now an array of feeders brings songbirds by the hundreds to our neighborhood. The river is also a flyway for ducks and geese, blue herons, and occasional eagles, and the woods are home to hawks and owls. There is perhaps more traffic here than in the city, but it's generally quieter; a little squawking from blue jays now and then, and the eerie music of coyotes in the evening, but otherwise little disturbs the silence.

We have given up a few things to live here: it has taken more effort to keep up on the music, theatre, and literary activities that we both love. And it certainly has cost us financially. But being here has repaid us a thousandfold in work that has had meaning to it, and in life enjoyed closer to the bone — or the earth, rather. If not a way to riches in dollars, the farm has been a way to live our lives far more fully than on the concrete surfaces of a city. ❧

RHG | *January 2010*

On the Farm

Haiku

Pointless dark scribbling.
Then, drawn to my light,
a Luna moth!
New poem!

'On the Farm, One Thing Leads to Another'

— E. B. WHITE

Started off this morning just to check the sugarbush
where yesterday I'd hung the buckets from their spiles
when the temperature in the sun rose to fiftyish
after a cool night and melted the last bit of
last week's snow, changing the season overnight to spring.

So I started up my Scout, old ugly plug of a woods car
and recently my plow for half a mile of township road
and thought, Well, I don't need the blade from here on in;
I'll drop that now, for driving in the snowless yard.

And did, except that where I drop it every spring,
out near the woodpile, there were logs I'd cut in fall,
in the very spot, uncut, unsplit; and then when I
had broken them, and fixed the starter on the saw that
broke its rope on the second pull,
and mounted up the splitter to the tractor,
stopping to fill that with gas; and after,
gathered chunks of broken wood to fill the rick, and
dropped some near the syrup cooker,
where I'd thrown junk wood
all last year — and then I saw the cooking pan was black
and needed scrubbing, or there was no point in starting
all of this at all.

RONALD GOWER

Now that shone scrubfaced clean, beside hoses snaked out
spitting chunks of ice and water finally coaxed
from the hydrant by the barn; and the plow blade lay powerless
where it would rest till fall;
chainsaw and tractor back in place, then hoses
coiled for garden soon to come;
and tire chains off the Scout
(an afterthought, an act of faith);
then down the field road rode,
riding light of winter but not of its old snow blended in the
murky earth so, halfway down, the Scout,
that sturdy chainless beast,
was deep beyond even its four-wheel clawing.

I started for the tractor, stopped, walked down first where
the sugarbush grew and sucked up sap in real spring
and where my buckets waved in Marching breeze, as empty
as the now-sunless air, too cool to coax lifeblood from earth
today, as empty as the hope that rises
in the chill of (very early) spring.
And noticed now the fat flakes starting slow,
that by the end of day would fill the woods and roads
and push back spring and sap and trembling life for weeks.

Maple Bend—I

It is not mine, I know.
My thirty years here
are just an instant,
just another line in
the scroll of owners
since this 17.92 acres
was defined and sold,
under Lincoln's hand,
"For the benefit of the
Winnebago," who
after all never
claimed to own it.
Nor do I, but for
this little time
it feels like home.
I've built and planted,
growing roots deep
in the black earth,
and for a while
lived and loved
this river island.
In another hundred
years my name will be
only one of dozens more.
It can be home just
for a moment
between ebb and flow
of the Maple River.

Maple Bend — II

Even this brings joy,
sitting in the bright circle
listening to the wolf-wind
keening over the world.

We are like piano strings
played by the current
that runs through it all.

In spring, the river
thrums with it, even
the earth vibrates.
It seems to hum:
"You are mine to
play softly, or break."

In gentler days,
we can feel the
new rhythm;
we plant our seed,
walk barefoot. Our
feet tingle, are warmed.

Now the music
has gone full cycle.
We are still here,
glad to be touched
by the old song.

Catching the Sun

Lightning bugs
bob over corn tassels
in the dark of late summer.
One touch: they burst
into flame.

They have gathered
the sun all day,
storing the fire inside,
invisible, waiting
for dark.

RONALD GOWER

Coyote on the River

It is bitter cold and clear,
a January Minnesota night,
and the little wolves begin
their symphony, their
Pathetique against what
loneliness or lament?

I see them seldom, but
know they live here,
keening ghosts of night
running grey on the
frozen river.

My springer is out
barking wildly at
the wildness in them
or him. He's not afraid
of them, doesn't want to
be part of the pack.
He's puzzled, doesn't
know what they are
that flow freely on the
ice and never seek
a home.

9N, D9

*Before we plow an unfamiliar patch it is well to be
informed about the winds, about the variations in the sky,
the native traits and habits of the place, what each locale
permits, and what denies.*   —VERGIL, *The Georgics*

My tough little Ford 9N
lurches, but lifts irresistibly,
and a whole wall of snow,
crusted conglomerate with
mud and ice, rises and rolls
like a wave, a corner
of the whole world before me.

It is easy to imagine
my neighbor's temptations:
given a longer lever, a huge
green JD or D9 Cat, he can move
and recreate the world,
flatten hills that slow the plow,
or gut a swamp, chase water
crying from the Eden of
flat and fallow cropping.

I drop the blade, release
what in my pride I've twisted
from its rest. Even the chains
leave marks that will last
until spring and beyond.

RONALD GOWER

Housemates

Another ladybug clings
to the inside of our bedroom door.
The outside is October.
I let it be, close it in
with us with the door I close
to the outside at night.

Some of our farmer friends
have dogs in the house.
Some we know of even have goats.
Not long ago, barn and house
had a shared wall: cattle-heat
warmed the humanpens as well.

But we stay separate,
most of the time: sheep, chickens,
dogs outside, undomestic,
and even the cats
live with us on the pretense
of being human.

But the lines often blur .
in the country, in October.
We try to warm each other,
and the small heat of creatures
is often closed in with us
for the autumn night.

Farmer

He seems so small beside
those great black bodies,
but is used to them,
prods them, shouts them
around, and they do
just what he says;
they are small inside.

I was driving an old loose
car once over a lumpy
dirt road, and everything
creaked, clanked, moved
in different directions.
That must be what the
inside of a cow
sounds like.

They seem to move
in sections, are slack-muscled,
but their heads are huge—
bulk of forehead between
eyes like dark lakes,
and some carry
blackhard horns.

They look dangerous,
but are only loosely hung
walking fields, meatracks;
they know nothing but
obedience and barns.

Fear of Animals

I.
We were bucking hay
— my hay for my goats —
but I worked feeling like a boy,
because he was the master here.
A real farmer, all his life, all he knew.
His hibibs didn't have to prove it:
his blood knew the seasons,
and his thick feet matched the ground.
So when he said,
"Out there in Wyoming
my daughter laughed like hell at me.
I went over that fence pretty quick
        for me.
She thought it was funny,
still kids me about it.
But, dammit,
        I don't trust a bull."
I was embarrassed and
had to say something.
"Well, they can get wild out there
        in all that prairie."
He wouldn't help himself or me:
"Oh, I don't even trust my own bull.
I raised him, of course,
and he knows me. But he's still got horns,
and he's so damn big.

Why, he could just break a man up.
Never has tried, probably never will.
          But I always watch him."

II.
Afterward, alone, it made me feel better.
Even my old billy has wicked eyes,
pupils like cough drops,
and his friendly prance
—ears back, hooves cocked—
has an edge to it.
And I have backed away from the snarl
and hard teeth set against blood-red
curl of gum on hackle-backed dogs.
I have plain turned and run, too,
from the swaying bulk of a black bear,
only a deeper shadow rolling my way
out of the black night of a forest camp.

III.
Cats live in our house.
They purr on the windowsills,
let us feed them and scratch their bellies.
They stalk lazily around
          and around and around us, every day.
I never turn my back on them,
especially.

Hunter's Eye

Like the poet, he senses
that almost imperceptible incongruity
marking the stark animal
against the otherwise
commonplace background,
the senseless surround.

Dark against light, white
thread in a dark weave, or
curve where all is timber-straight,
and most almost the mystical
sense of something vital
where the rest rests.

The test, then, is to capture it
before just that sensed image
becomes startled life, gathering
into itself and becoming just
the fleeing creature, quickly lost
in the forest printed in the eye.

RONALD GOWER

Among the Carnivores

It is easy to tell the fox tracks,
for they are always in a straight line,
one foot before the other.
            —— BOY SCOUT HANDBOOK

When I stop to rest,
I see my footprints stretching
out behind me in a line,
all the way home.

Deer tracks decorate
my cutting line,
curving round like oxbows
in a stream.

Mine, like the arrows I carry,
point downstream, purposeful,
bloodlust at their pointed ends,
where curve and line converge.

Into the Woods

This is not the forest primeval,
just a stand of woods between
river and farmland, too much
trouble to cut down and plow.
There are roads nearby, and
I sit in a stand only half a mile
from my truck.

Still, as it grows dark, I grow
uneasy, though I still hope
for the buck that might wander
within range of my bow.
I'm twelve feet up a tree,
I'm seventy years old, and
my heart is still pounding
from the walk in.

All the what-ifs start:
a dizzy spell, a fall, the chance,
though slim, that I'll get lost.
I almost leave, though it's early.
But then I hear a rustle of leaves
and am outside myself again.

RONALD GOWER

It's nothing: a squirrel, a late bird.
Still, the moment of panic passes.
I will, after all, die somewhere,
and this melting into the woods
would not be the worst of ends.

That, or making the final fall
into a trout stream, feeling the
cold for only a moment, and then
drifting with the current, down
and down, returning home.

Some Would Call It Junk

Pieces of old machines, or
machines scavenged of other
pieces: ends of pipes, boards,
sheet metal left from other jobs,
and rope, chain, belts, straps,
and string, seldom too short
to be saved.

If it were not of value,
would it be stacked and stored
in piles, on shelves, in drawers,
and, yes, sometimes where it fell?

Well, I tell you, when you live
out here, a dozen miles from
plumbers, electricians, carpenters,
and all the tradefolk carrying
new junk in their shiny trucks,
a piece of rusty wire may be
all that holds a fenceline tight
and convinces a brainless lamb
to spend the night with you
instead of finding a river to
fall into; or chain may be
the link, the length to reach
from tractor-back to sunken truck,
grounded in snow or muck.

RONALD GOWER

I can throw things away,
the clutter that seems just then
just that, the useless detritus
that will not fit a shelf and
could not be of any use
and that is junk; you can
call it that — if you ever
find it, because I never
throw it far, and that one time
I'll need a broken hose,
scrap of heavy leather
inches wide, or broken post
to stiffen concrete slab,
I'll know just where it is.

The string? That goes around
a finger and reminds me twice:
that old boot sole is there,
in the fissure by the creek,
half-buried by the hose and
post and perfect junk
in exile till its time.
And the string is a reject,
almost thrown away, to be
my reminder to throw
nothing too far away.

Goat Proem

I started with goats a year ago
— two summers and a winter, really —
and only one goat the same the whole time.
That first summer I bought two kids,
male and female, unrelated, I was assured.
They were supposed to keep the weeds down
on a couple of acres of hillside I owned.
I made a corral a hundred feet across,
and built a small shed.
By the middle of July,
they were twice as big,
and the space inside my fence
was like erosion in the green hill,
like a bomb crater; they ate down to dirt,
then started working on that and the shed.

So I fenced all I owned with woven wire —
two hundred by six hundred, four feet high,
straight down the hill, through the raspberries,
sweating and mosquito-bit; then
straight up the hill on the other end.
I turned them loose in August,
rolling up the corral, not knowing
what to do with all the extra fence.

They started right away doing
what they do best:
getting out of fences.

I spent the rest of the summer and fall
finding where I'd been careless,
tightening loose wire and posts,
and adding a top row
—one strand of barbed wire
all the way around—
then sitting back to wait
until they escaped again.

With winter coming on,
I built a new shed for them,
dug it deep into the hillside,
made a pole frame, and piled straw bales
all around: a snug cave, snow-covered soon.
Then I found out what they do next best:
the doe was pregnant, and she'd kid
right in mid-winter.

I traded her to a farmer-friend,
traded her for his old billy
that he didn't want around anyway,
now that the does were all pregnant enough.
So all winter I had bachelors' camp out there,
two now-full-sized billies
living like trolls in the hill-cave.
They weren't going anywhere,
not in mid-winter.
What they did instead, to pass the time,

was to kick down the shed:
they were too smart to play cards, or smoke,
and had all winter on their hooves.
Every time I came out,
there'd be a side missing; they stood around,
complaining about the cold.
I built the shed back, put woven wire all around,
hammered it to the poles:
they pulled the nails out, somehow,
and walked through another wall.

As if that weren't enough,
they wanted to eat more or less always.
I'd bought fifty bales of alfalfa hay,
stored it in the neighbor's barn,
and every three days I'd throw one of them.
Miss a day, they'd start eating their shed.
I didn't miss many days, not even
when we had the big blizzard
and I had to ski in carrying their feed.

After the storm, the snow was drifted high,
especially along my fences.
As soon as it was wind-hardened enough,
they walked up one side of a drift
and down and out the other.
I had a call from my neighbor, the first time:
they were in his garage, eating tires.
So it was back to the fences again,
where the snow was high, and digging away ramps.

When spring finally came, my fence melted up,
eight feet high in places,
woven wire stacked on wire.
And in the warm and wet of spring,
their blood thawed, and their balls.
Even old Joe squirted jism everywhere,
would have humped a stump
if it had a hole in it.
And stink! The smell built all summer,
like another animal,
till you could smell goat from the road.
And with lots of range, billies get fussy:
the weeds grew thick, but they ate nothing
but all the tree leaves they could reach, and the bark.
My hillside looked like a swamp
full of peeled cattails, like a
whole army of beavers gone berserk
in the woods.
They ate everything I wanted left
— grapevines, pines, chokecherry, maple —
and left all the plantain, itchweed,
even the juicy raspberry tangles,
strictly alone.

They got lonesome, too.
Both were full goats now
and tired of butting heads,
playing ram-of-the-herd with no herd.
So they started over, six feet tall on hind legs,
walking up and over the fence anytime.

I added another row of barbed wire,
all the way around, and waited, and added.
Finally, I put them on long chains,
untangled them every day,
and waited for winter.

But after winter
—and that'll be bad enough—
spring will come, it always has,
and I can't expect it to change its ways
just because I have two billy goats.
They're the biggest animals I've ever owned.

I sit home nights thinking about them.

I haven't had many animals, being a city boy.
I did have a cute tiny lamb once, but it died.
I remember I gave it a big funeral,
a real grave, and I cried a lot.
I'm sure goats don't die, ever.

Northern Winter

In old New Mexico, cloudy days
were like a Two-Grey-Hills blanket,
blessed shelter and brief relief
from constancy of light,
quick curtain blink before the play
began again, sun always center stage.

Here in Minnesota, cloud is like
a tucked-in billowing sheet,
sky-wide and infinitely long;
the sun does not exist, or sleeps
all winter on the clouds, except
as a far distant star, blind and cold
as forty white degrees below.

When once winter lifts,
all rushes up, wet mist of cloud
and melt thrust up through
stick and stem, bursts into leaf
and spills its sap into my spiles.

It is this dawn at last, an eye opening
after long dark, that keeps us here,
who were too stunned with desert's
constant blaze, that single note.

Walking on Snakeskin

I want to get to the other side,
explore the hills over there, the trees
and the tiered field disked delicately
into terraces below the woods.

Between here and there the ice is rotten,
has snow and water stripes on it,
and the black snake's muscles winding
below the white skin.
I am afraid of them.

If this were a lake, had a turtle shell,
I would not hesitate, would not
carry a stick and heavy rock.
There if the shell cracks
I have only to grab an edge,
pull straight up to the air.

Here there is that coiled thing,
the live wicked muscle that would pull me
below the mottled skin, rip away air
in its quick flex.
I walk slowly across, trembling my way,
holding my stick crossed against fear
and throwing the rock before me,
listening for the sound of striking.

RONALD GOWER

In the Gap

So here we sit
in a house with logs in it
on a river-bottom farm
here a hundred years.
And how do you think,
old man, part of this?

There is a different thing
happening behind your eyes.
Whatever it is I think
I know
it is something else.
Even your silence
is different,
is no darker
than your words.

Down the Road

First Snow

It ends with one prophetic day,
bitter around the edges,
the last autumn warmth
slipping away.

Bare dark trees point
into a grey sky,
bony fingers reaching
for a far distant sun:

*It will come
from there, from the moon,
turning the brown grass lunar,
burying the corpse of gardens,
and we will be the only
testimonial to life to come.*

Ahab

He was crazy, on that at least we can agree.
Never mind the symbols, or even that he started out
with perfectly sane revenge in mind. After all,
Moby had smashed him and nipped off a leg, to boot.
Never mind all that: what explains him is madness.
Anyone who gives up gold and reputation, self-respect
and more whale oil is crazy, right?
And usually dead.

Yet here I am again, knowing that, grinding along
the long of Duluth, sharpening my harpoon.
I have left work at home undone,
will return stubbled, cold, red-eyed and foul,
and probably oil-less: the steelhead always win.
Six years and no fish, yet here I am come spring.
And they have only torn line from my numb hands,
never even nibbled off a toe.
One of these years, they'll find me
webbed in monofilament,
spreadeagled like Gregory Peck.

But it's spring. The Knife and the Brule churn brown,
and I know a great trout turns its head
toward the smell of flood under the ice
and glows white up dark waters.

Wilderness

On a late lamp-lit walk,
I feel a hot stare from the dark,
beyond the civilized tar,
am suddenly chilled as a large
night-grey dog crosses
silently to intercept my step.
I stop cold, have my gentle
intentions sniffed, and am
dismissed disinterestedly
to walk on at ease,
but feel a tingle
in my spine.

It is good to keep dogs
around in the dark,
and stiff-backed cats
are better still.
They remind us to walk
carefully between the streets
and the dark edges.

The Interstices

This is a very small town, with few old buildings left,
and most of them show cracks and chinks from years
of life, and horses gone to cars, cobble streets to tar,
and the commotion of a thousand people riding,
walking, eating, fighting, loving in the open space
inside and out of what still stands after birth and death.

Thousands lived here for a hundred years, and some
are still alive, five hundred, more or less, but all the rest
are here as well, in those cracks and chinks of memory,
buildings, homes, farms named after faceless ghosts,
grudges still held, though the cause and even those
who first crossed words in anger at that cause are gone.

The history of anywhere is not the history written down;
it is the web of loves and hates, of wives who run away,
of men who kill a farm, or drown in drink, or children who
escape, to not become their parents' shadow in the town
which has decided early what they are and always will be.
It is the thing that lives in cracks and chinks of buildings,
and in the spaces in between the living and the dead.

Midwesterners Not Watching an Eclipse

There has been a storm,
but now the clouds are gone.
It stands out stark in
that rain-clean sky,
being chewed up slowly
by the dark behind the world.
This one night in thousands
it will do a sleight-of-hand
on itself, lose its own daylight.

No one sees.
Midwestern towns form their own
lakes of light
out on the prairies
between cornfield continents,
and cars like water bugs
speed by on small
midnight romances.
They beep familiarly
as they pass.
Only the dogs notice,
howl up at miracles
bigger than themselves.

We Live by Myths, and Die

Near Mankato, Minnesota,
there is a junction
called Nine-Mile Corner,
where people in cars go
to kill themselves, regularly,
smashing both into junk and jelly.

It would not be a dangerous place,
except that everyone now knows
it is a dangerous place.
I think if no one had first
quite by accident
died there, cars would go
about minding their own business,
as if it were only another
pair of concrete slabs
meeting by a stop sign.

But since it is now
Nine-Mile Corner,
ghosted by one primal crash,
then another, and more
imitating the act of death —
my fingers tighten
coming there, and the car sways.
I work to keep it right
of the sinister center,
the white life-line.

RONALD GOWER

On Seeing Magpies Again
and Knowing I Have Come West

It is a special kind of Western bravery
that will not be solemn over death.
The magpie lives at funerals, wears black,
but this will not make its life a long mourning,
like crows: he will not fly that somber way,
but travel with a swoop and flip,
a long sword-thrust of tail, and over black
a panache of bold white, daring death
even as he searches for it
along the concrete rivers,
where the killers never eat their kill.

The world is full of blood here.
Life is the exception, and life must
face that terror always there at its feet.
And so to live is to make denial,
show life in its harlequin coat,
or the joke on Twain's lips
that keeps the bitterness covered
like a pool of suncrusted blood.

Making Love to a New Town

They're not all alike, despite
McDonald's and Wal-Mart, and
each town has its charms and its
warts, and it's like getting to know
a new woman: Will I like her?
Will she like me? What is she
all about?

She shows me her charms,
proud of them, but shy and wary:
I am still strange to them
and cannot come close too fast.

I see an old opera house,
a bank by Sullivan, houses painted
in Acadian rainbow hues, a basketball
court for a Mexican plaza, live oak trees
as old as the world, even castles perched
distant from the village
they once protected.

But these are signs and symbols,
and it is in the small cafés and bars
and shops and plazas where I find
the real soul, the intimate biography
of each, and the words that hint
of history, of blood ties and bloody
grudges, gossip, and politics.

RONALD GOWER

And I must learn quickly in what
language to woo her; not English,
Spanish, French, but in attitudes
assumed, distances kept
one from another,
what words will bring
a tentative smile, a closing down.

In the Mojave

This living in the sky
all the time
makes one feel like
some part of a god.

Not *The*: this has
nothing to do with
a shackling church
but the prayer
between a Zia sun
and feet buried in sand,
with filling in the space
between. Not
the scent of candles
but of hot live sage
and piñon that turn
somewhere in skin
and sweat to the scent
of a heaven hung
between earth and sky.

Pueblo

The center stands here
in the kiva
a surface shimmer of
old drought, Apache, and
conquistador, priests
and quakes and even Anglo
unnatural machine and
pop can culture—
all wash over
wrinkling surfaces
perhaps even turned to
new kachina alongside
all the ancient ones,
but all flowing over
eventually, inevitably.
And deep down
the kiva root remains
as it was
as it has been
as it will be.

Zihuatanejo

It is like coming back
to an old love, after
a long journey.
She has waited
without impatience,
changing little,
as familiar and strange
as always.

She is the city of women,
where men once
went to sea escaping war,
leaving a town of queens.
The men still leave each day,
and each night on the Bahia
the women allow them
their homes, admire
their fruit from the sea.

They live somewhere
between beach and sea
in the warm peace of
the music, lilies,
basketball courts,
the rough streets and
the calm waters
of the Bahia
that ebb and flow
only a little each day.

RONALD GOWER

The Way of Trout

How to explain that
it must be this way,
unless it is only
in this way
to walk in beauty.

It is all ritual,
and the crafted
fly must be a
perfect song
to walk in beauty.

The water is
a sheet of music
with no notes,
but you must read
to walk in beauty.

A piece of water
breaks, a note
turns solid fire,
perfect music,
as you walk in beauty.

Trout too catch fire,
sing, hook in lip,
send music up
the line and rod
to end in beauty.

Alchemy — I

Part of the river is fish.
If I can turn it to
a sliver of bright life,
water turned quicksilver,
aimed up to where
the river splits by the
alchemy of hunger,
it will find that fly
that is not a fly, that too
has changed from
something else,
a shimmering mayfly
with a steel spine.

Alchemy—II

A piece of water
twists off, becomes
quicksilver, both fire
and muscle aimed
for killing.

Trout, too, catch fire,
mouth to flame,
feather to steel,
and the throb
like heat reaches
through line and rod.

Off the Lip

No apologies
are possible
in the demanding
now
of rock tree mogul
ice powder
pull.
Now is just
obedience
to the task-
master fall line
down
screaming
look move thrust
look hold no
now
look check now
singing
down now
yes

RONALD GOWER

Climax

Skiing powder
is like
the last shuddering
thrust of love
when there is no time
when there is no thought
no choice
no fear
and the straight plunge
down is certain ecstasy
and the one
is lost
folded in passion
in union
in the soft white thighs
of the beloved.

Après-ski

After
the day's poetry
scribbled savagely
in the snow
we settle uneasily
to the soft
and too-warm
prose echoes.

RONALD GOWER

Ullr

Just rarely
on some few mountains
it all comes back.
The distraction
the noisy attraction
of people subtracted.
You come face to face
with his rock strength
and chill pine-sweet
breath of song
with the threat the thrill
of his dangerous love.

You caress the
cool white skin
of your enemy lover
wanting his cruel smile
and song of sighs
fearing his icy claws
but matching his
raw passion
in your giddy plunge
and remember ecstasy
on some lone mountains.

Living at the Peak

We can learn something about it
watching the meticulous mountain climber:
he looks right before his eyes,
finds the solid handholds and cracks,
rams in pitons where they'll catch,
anchors himself only to good rock—
and then when he moves, thinks of nothing,
but concentrates each muscle, breath, nerve,
ounce into the next step,
and never, ever looks down.

He lives with fear,
within his skill,
doing calmly what
only seems impossible.

And on the way may
either fall, quietly
and with the same
deliberation,
or make his way
all the way
in perfect awareness.

Fishing Late on the Whitewater

Even the bright water
is turning dark,
but there are
circles and swirls
here and there,
and I throw
a blind fly
toward them.
It is hard to stop
this late.

I have waded
in sunlight all day.
All seventy years.
And now in shadow
I feel the current
pulse and pull
on my legs.
It wants me
to go with it,
sink into the dark,
see finally the
hovering forms
beneath the surface.

D'ou venons-nous? Que sommes-nous?
Ou allons-nous?

— PAINTING BY PAUL GAUGUIN

They are becoming familiars,
the old easy formalities
with which we say our
last farewells.

Each one is easier than the last,
the sickle edge growing blunt.
The first ones cut so deep,
hurt so hard.

Is this too grave; another way
of forgetting, avoiding
what little we do
know of life?

We come from shadows,
we go into the dark.
In between
a brief touching.

Face to Face at Last

Two old men sit
in their cracked veins
detailing ache and remedy
for bodies gone worthless
and so precious vessels now.
And more, both wonder
underneath: can that
pure child I knew
be ruined inside, too?

They look at each other
secretly suspicious
as at carnival mirrors
and wonder if this
is really still them
and if any germ
any immortal gem
could still survive
time's terrible corruption.

Another Death on the Highway

How we think
at all
at our speed
is miraculous,
and then
what do I do
with a poem
ripe in my womb
at 70 MPH?

Signs say
NO STOPPING EXCEPT
IN AN EMERGENCY
and it is
but
how explain
to a cop
I stopped for a
nativity
here, alone?

Would he
hold off the world
with siren and shield,
and then
what if
nothing showed but
inky afterbirth

still-born
in siren-glare?
Or how explain,
"It's a bouncing baby
sonnet — preemie,
ten lines, no tail,
purple eyes"?
That would be when
I'd be truncheoned
insensible
for being a
loaded weapon
without a license.

No.
I let go
at 70 MPH
and the bloody babe,
slips out,
tears loose
umbilical memory,
and is gone,
lost in the
concrete instant.

Jade Mountain Illustrating
the Gathering of Poets
at the Lan T'ing Pavilion, 353 AD

— MINNEAPOLIS ART INSTITUTE

The *Jade Mountain* glows softly,
throwing all else into shadow.
I am drawn to it each time, and
find nothing else I wish to see
as much.

I think of poetry gatherings
in America, in the 20th century,
and how even at the foot of
Mount Hui-chi, there were surely
some who sipped too much sake
from their saucers, and certainly
young students were seduced.
And, for sure, there was shouting
over those radicals who played
fast and loose with classical forms,
or drew characters too hastily, or
tried to bend them to their will
and want.

And yet, from all that clash
of libido and ego, fire and
ink, idea and will,
rose *Jade Mountain,*
rose the voices chanting
song into the pale green night
at Lan T'ing, Amherst, or
Paterson, New Jersey.

Laius in His Chariot

I.

It is a bad dream, and I am sweating.
I know it is a dream, and I reserve the right
to wake up, but I want to see what happens.
Then I am into it, and forget:
I hunt for a man who is trying to kill me.
I sweat through a black jungle,
carrying my hunting bow and razor arrows.
There is one of those powerless dream-fights:
I strike and strike, tremble and weaken.
Finally, an arrow goes home, my dark enemy falls.
It is my son. His vomit of blood
in my quaking arms wakes me.

II.

I am driving home after work.
I see a boy walking the same way:
I know it is Him. How I know
I don't know, for he is taller
than in my house. He walks like
all boys, only unlike adults:
they wander, things go up from them
and are caught, streets do not
fit their shoes. Yet he is himself,
not like others whose shape he is like
or whose walk.

When I stop the car beside him, he looks surprised.
Another green world falls out of his eyes,
   as I trap him in the family car and carry him home,
   a deer that would otherwise escape my arrow.

Myownhorn

When I was young I was forced to take
piano lessons, which I hated until I
didn't have to take them, after
which I loved to play piano.

And I played and played and played
until one day when I was older I
heard George Shearing do the
same thing, only not,
and I knew I
was just
playing.

I loved the sound of jazz trombone,
so I learned how to breathe again
and how to fill that plumbing
full of air, and make it slip
and slide, and then at the
Prom Ballroom, I
heard Tommy
Dorsey.

RONALD GOWER

Next day I picked up an old guitar,
and for the next three years I
worked to harden fingertips,
to strum and stroke and
make it sing, and this
is it, I thought, until
an old man named
Segovia walked
across the frets
like an angel
from hell
and

That was that.
Now I think I
will just make
something else
and patent it
and no one else
will be allowed
but me to blow.

Poet 007

I.
Here I am, a poet with a shotgun,
sitting in an Iowa tavern
drinking beer,
surrounded by
other hunters.
What would they do
if they knew?

II.
Later, at the airport,
they too suspect,
but can do nothing:
I am undetected by machines,
by airline vigilantes.
And I am a canny spy,
sneak on board
a whole imaginary arsenal
of skyrockets and sparklers
and other mostly
harmless explosives,
cloaking mystery and nonregulation,
blank bullets of fantasy
inside my dangerous
bald luggage.

III.
My cover is blown,
and the situation now
is life or death.
I reveal myself,
sign page after page
of the evidence.
It will be either
the sneer of shotguns,
or applause, or worse,
no one will notice.

Peer Gynt

The silence of inward spaces
terrifies me:
One acts, one is — the infinite
outside is evidence.
Yet if I stop moving an instant,
my eyes roll back,
and I am blinded
by that awful emptiness.

So one lives and moves,
banging his husk noisily
against the world,
carefully not thinking
of nothing happening.

RONALD GOWER

Metamorphosis

In the glare of spotlights
across the immense bare stage
an old bald round drab man
shuffles his way to a chair
ignoring the familiar thunder.
He squats gracelessly, belly
slung between his thighs,
ignoring the silence also
and his body, knowing these
have nothing to do with
Segovia.

An unfurling of sound
and before our eyes
Segovia appears, the
slim blond prince, black
burning matador, hawk,
dove, nightingale, cecropia
of the misty night, as he
unwraps his soul and lets
it walk the frets,
looking like fingers.

A Sullen Choice

I can't wait to get old:
I will be an evil, dirty old man
carrying a wicked, gnarled cane —
an old man full of bad habits
grown as carefully as weeds.

And I will do exactly as I want.
I will not change my socks
or shirt or pants or even underwear.
Ever.

I will not work, especially not
at good deeds.
I will be an anti-Boy Scout
and form a new pack of
Dirty Old Men Scouts.
A bad deed every day.
Girls will not stir me any more,
and I will pull their pigtails,
or grey buns, and sneer
at their tears.

I will do exactly as I want —
things children can never do.
And since I cannot be a child again,
I cannot wait to be
a dirty old man
with a twisted stick.

RONALD GOWER

Burnout

My son has a real talking doll:
pull its cord
and some complex machine
lets out a length of sound,
different each time and now
overused, in chaotic order.
It reminds me of me,
to quote John Wayne.
Pull the string coded Shelley
and get fifty minutes —
exactly, there's the bell,
period — of mechanical
romantic sound
without fury or significance.
And in this dull doll factory,
where one builds into oneself
a suicide of mind by mouth,
I see myself performing
thus, on cue, until
the whole machine destructs,
or the grooves grow so dull
no one hears,
or no one pulls my cord,
or until
the wrong sounds blurt out
at the wrong times
like my son's
deranged doll.

Déjà Vieux

In my recurring dream,
the draft has come for me
again, and I am whisked
to basic training, despite
my wail at every stage
that I am now seventy
and surely not a soldier
any more.

And then I'm crawling
through Fort Carson mud
and carrying a combat pack
filled for a giant, plus my old
MI, and metal helmet, and
the weight of fifty years
since as a 'Cruit E-I it all was
just a game.

The heaviness this time
is that I know what follows,
know the rules, and when
the rules go wrong: the
right way and the Army way,
and that that machine gun is not
firing at a cautious line
above my head.

RONALD GOWER

I die, of course, this time,
and I know that, too, that
two is an unlucky number.
This time I will not have
those fifty years forgetting
or those times when I
remember, when I hope
in my dream it is
only a dream.

Leaving

My old friend has gone beyond emotion,
past the value of objects or even words
to a place I cannot follow just now.

His books line shelves, buried
under the dust of his mind,
lost somewhere in broken synapses.

An old lamp lies on the floor
as if dead, forgotten, or
unnoticed where it fell.

Cigarette butts and pills, car keys
and stale food, scotch tape and
pennies crust over the single table

where he sits, shedding ashes,
moving only to suck the smoke
and listen to the swirl in his head,

the echo of the lightning bolts that
snapped lines, set flame to
fragile webs of memory and name,

RONALD GOWER

staring at the clutter, but seeing
only inside, where things still move
at random, lamps and images of love.

He waits among piles of bills and poems
for the next thing to happen to him
about which he thinks and cares very little.

I've Known Women

Yes, I have,
and loved lots of them lots.
The beauties at first sight,
their animal grace or
perfect face reason enough,
prey expecting to be chased,
and I was always willing
to scent after them, kneel
before their glowing,
and adore.

The vixens, arms akimbo,
tongues of knives and
swaying skirts, the Carmens
of their tribe; oh, they are
lovely, lusty things, pure
spirit of the urge that
burned me in their heat.

Then last and best,
the gentle, pretty
freckled girl, who speaks
directly, low and slow,
and listens, too, as if
there is no pretty game,
and she not a player in the
bend and bow and riposte

RONALD GOWER

making boy and girl
two different things.

For she will, with a word,
or open smile,
not sly or languorous, or
with unconscious touch,
without a trace of haste;
or in a moment's grace
in some small act
grow beautiful before
my eyes, a woman human,
as I am a man, and not
a picture or a flame.

And never after, as I
roam the world with her,
can she be less than
most beautiful, less than
herself, who in an instant
tuned my senses
to a deeper pitch.

Two of the Many Kinds of Love

With men and women,
love thrives on separation,
meetings and leavings that leave
lovers unsatiate, yearning
for more than they really
may want, unless it is really

with a man and a woman
love, which grows out of
the familiar, the common smells,
the touch that means not always
a quickening, but often only
a warm reminder, and the feel
gentler than the fire that began it —
that the leaving now always
will mean return, and
it does not burn to touch
or part.

RONALD GOWER

The Sadness of Men With No Songs

We have no long songs
no chants spirit-freighted
to pass on, men to boys,
fathers to sons.

These are not heroic
times, nor can we lie
as lyres often did, to
mend our pettiness.

There are no voices
rumbling by campfires
while boy-men struggle
with their eyes.

We sit silent
in the ashes,
can give voice to
nothing worth time
or song
or passing on.

The Taste of Ashes

We are driving back now from a lunch and talk
with friends, my father's friends, and the talk,
the Governor's talk,
was of my father's goodness, because
he was dead there.
He is done there now, finished,
everyone is done with him.

Except my father's bones rattle in the trunk.
We ignore them, the live ones talking up here,
his get, driving, riding, talking—
but I hear them rattle back there,
almost swear at them as I talk, so as not to.

His real bones no longer are anywhere,
only one more belch
from a dirty smokestack,
a few darker spots more
in the black scurf of the city.
If they are here, right here,
they may drift down like black snow,
or be drowned in the black rain
falling over us.

The inside of the car keeps darkening.
I am afraid of the dark talk
against that, too. Only the children
accept the ashes, wish him well,
wise enough not to have heard him
for forty years.

In the trunk is his exoskeleton,
uncremate, rattling around on nerves:
pipes he chewed, tennis racket, armor
for that last soft flesh
burning one last time now,
no longer needed and also on its own.

The World Behind Us

He is six and learning words,
words in books.
It is hard work.
His tongue juts out
like a small animal
as he sounds letters,
looks at new black marks.

At night, when he is asleep,
his mother leads him
into the bathroom.
He is out cold,
walking between her legs.

"Frud" he pronounces clearly,
eyes still closed.
"All right, Frud."
"Uz," he is satisfied.
He pees, is taken back.
He falls on the bed,
back into his own book.

Taking It With Me

When they dig my tomb
I want the riches of a Tut
around me, treasures and
story of my own life,
clutched in my last grasp,
brought to the grave, viz:

One fine double gun,
loaded and ready;
my best Fenwick rod
and flies that do not
buzz; books that will
last — Dickinson and
Walt and Will — and
for a mark, one lock
of Anne's hair.

No gold piece on my
watchchain, please,
although silver dollars
on my eyes
would be nice.
Not to pay the freight, but
blinding me to
a heaven without senses
that holds none of the above
at value.

Mu ("Unask the Question")

We learn so late that
so many things we learned
were wrong, were learned
because parents learned
what they had learned
was wrong, and turned.

So two rights make
another wrong, and
the right for you
only your grandson
will learn is right for
him when it is too late.

RONALD GOWER

Living It Inarticulate

God, all the marvelous
poems
I never wrote!
Just to know them
was to love them
though
as they say.
But there was
never time to pause
to package them
in words before
life intruded with
yet another marvel
more jolts of wonder
another unworded
poem.

Acknowledgments

I wish to thank *County Lines* for permission to reprint "The Way of Trout." Other poems in this collection have appeared in *The Cream City Review, Loonfeather Magazine, North Country Anvil, Oxygen, Poetic License, Stardust and Fate: The Blueroad Reader, Talking Stick, Twin Cities Magazine,* and *Willow Avenue Review.*

My deepest thanks to Cary Waterman, student, teacher, friend, and master poet for her editing and advice; to John and Abbey Gaterud, the most skillful and generous publishers one could hope for; and to my best friend, Anne, the love of my life, and our boys, Owen and Hugh, who have all put up with my "craft and sullen art" these many years.

Thanks also to longtime friend, hunting partner, and journalist John Cross, for the magical cover photo, "Morning Drink." Like the protagonist in "Hunter's Eye," John can turn an everyday moment into fine art.

逆

The Author

© John Cross

Ron Gower grew up in South St. Paul, and is a professor emeritus of Minnesota State University, Mankato, where he taught primarily American literature, including Canadian and South American courses. He has also been a soldier, ski instructor, musician, and freelance writer. His publications include literary criticism, essays and features, and more than one hundred poems, but this is his first book of poetry.

෴

Colophon

This text in this book is set in Adobe Garamond Pro, Robert Slimbach's 1989 digital rendering of the roman types of Claude Garamond and the italic types of Robert Granjon. The book's titles are set in Helvetica LT Std, designed by Alfred Hoffmann with Max Miedinger in 1957.

❦

WHEN LION
COULD FLY